IMAGES
of America

CALDWELL
COUNTY

According to legend, these intertwined poplar trees bear silent testimony to a treaty between the Catawba and Cherokee Indians. The Catawba lived primarily in South Carolina and Georgia, with Union and Mecklenberg Counties as the northern limits of their traditional boundaries. The Cherokee claimed a great deal of Western North Carolina as traditional hunting ground. The Catawba and Cherokee clashed on a number of occasions. The legend contends that in 1737, after a particularly brutal battle in which the warriors of both tribes were decimated, the two groups erected a pile of stones to mark their boundary line and tied together two young poplars to indicate their desire for future peace between the tribes. Unfortunately, despite this beautiful symbol, the Catawba and Cherokee tribes fought again in 1760 and in 1776 during the American Revolution. The trees, known as the "Twin Poplars," remain, though the Catawba and Cherokee are long gone. They stand in Warriors' Gap off U.S. 321. (Caldwell.)

ON THE COVER: Due to the influenza epidemic of 1918–1919, all public meetings, including school, were canceled. So that they could graduate on time, the Lenoir High seniors met in the bank building. Students from this unusual class are pictured from left to right with a Lenoir fire truck: (on the ground) Carolyn Poe, Reginald May, Ruth Crisp, Fred Dula, and Mavis Goodman; (in the truck) Mary Dula, Mamie Walton, Florrie Wilson, Alice Robbins, Nell Killiam, Dwight Blackwelder, Ruth White, Faith Courtney, Hallie Lenoir, Charles Jones, Edward Covington, and Oscar Peirce. (Caldwell.)

IMAGES
of America

CALDWELL
COUNTY

Michael C. Hardy

ARCADIA
PUBLISHING

Published by Arcadia Publishing
Charleston, South Carolina

Library of Congress Catalog Card Number: 2006931307

For all general information contact Arcadia Publishing at:
Telephone 843-853-2070
Fax 843-853-0044
E-mail sales@arcadiapublishing.com
For customer service and orders:
Toll-Free 1-888-313-2665

Visit us on the Internet at www.arcadiapublishing.com

*The author would like to dedicate this book to the many families
and individuals who, over the years, have generously donated
photographs and other items to the Caldwell Heritage Museum.
Because of these donations, future generations will be able to see,
touch, and understand Caldwell's diverse and fascinating history.*

CONTENTS

ACKNOWLEDGMENTS

The author would like to thank the following, who donated items for consideration for this project (the notations following each name will serve as photograph courtesy lines) Wayne Beane (Beane), Gary Corley (Corley), Mary Adelaide Dula (Dula), Caldwell Heritage Museum (Caldwell), Randy Gibson (Gibson), Ed Greene (Greene), Michael C. Hardy (Hardy), Doris Holloway (Holloway), Anne Stowe Hsu (Hsu), Betsy McRee (McRee), the Patterson School (Patterson), Charles Lafayette Smith (Smith), Mary Throneburg (Throneburg), and Brenda Triplett (Triplett). Special thanks goes to the staff and volunteers of the caldwell Heritage Museum and to my readers, John Hawkins and Elizabeth Baird Hardy.

This group of veterans is gathered at a reunion in Lenoir, Caldwell County. They proudly display small Army of Northern Virginia battle flags, and some of the old soldiers are wearing reunion medals. Men from Caldwell County served in the 22nd North Carolina, 26th North Carolina, and 58th North Carolina regiments. (Caldwell.)

INTRODUCTION

When William Lenoir walked out beyond the Rip Shin Mountains and gazed north, he was looking at the frontier of America. For many years, everything north of the crest of the Blue Ridge was off-limits to white settlers. It was not until the late 1700s that the area of the once-dominant Cherokee was opened to settlement.

Following the end of the American Revolution, others settlers began to pour into the region at the foothills of the Blue Ridge. They came seeking a prosperous future where land could be had, homes built, and families raised. The fertile valleys between the Yadkin and Catawba Rivers fit their desires. However, life was still dangerous here. Fort Defiance, the Keyhole House, and other new homes built in the area between the rivers were constructed with loopholes or gun ports so settlers could defend their families.

Still others came to join the Lenoirs, including the Littlejohn, Blair, Baird, Deal, Jones, and Laxton families. By the late 1830s, there were enough families in the area to begin talking about forming a separate county. The lawmakers in Raleigh were petitioned, and in 1841, the new county was formed, named Caldwell in honor of Dr. Joseph Caldwell, the first president of the University of North Carolina.

Ten years passed between the formation of Caldwell County and the incorporation of a county seat. Property that had once belonged to the Tucker family was purchased and named Lenoir in honor of Maj. Gen. William Lenoir. Ten more years passed before the greatest test America has yet faced broke upon the nation. And when the Civil War split the nation in two, Caldwell County men joined the Southern armies in droves. They joined some of the most famous regiments in Confederate history, such as the 26th North Carolina Troops. This regiment, at the Battle of Gettysburg, was in the thickest of the fight on two of the battle's three days. Company F, made up of Caldwell County boys, went into the fight with 91 men. Of those men, 19 were killed and 72 wounded, 12 mortally, a casualty rate of 100 percent.

Caldwell County sent men to fight in the western theater of the war as well. Companies E and H of the 58th North Carolina Troops, fought at Chickamauga, Lookout Mountain, and in the battles for Atlanta. At Bentonville, this regiment was under the command of Maj. George W. F. Harper, a Caldwell County native and a business leader after the war.

Progress was slow in coming to Caldwell County following the end of the war. As in many other communities all across the South, the war had devastated the local economy and workforce. It also was no help that the first railroad to enter Western North Carolina bypassed Caldwell County to the south. The Western North Carolina Railroad had almost reached Morganton by 1861, but construction came to a halt when the war began.

As time passed, outside investors soon set their eyes on the virgin tracts of timber that lay within Western North Carolina. While timbering had been practiced on a small scale, it took a railroad for major timber harvesting to begin. In 1884, the Chester and Lenoir Railroad reached the county seat. This was a narrow gauge line that approached the county from the south. After reaching Lenoir, a new line branched out to the north. Called the Carolina and Northern, this line cut a path into the mountains and terminated in the new mill town of Edgemont in 1894.

The arrival of the railroad ushered in a time of unprecedented prosperity for the citizens of Caldwell County. The first furniture manufacturer, Harper Furniture Company, was established in 1889. Other furniture companies, such as Moore Furniture County, the Hudson Cotton Mill, and the Kent Furniture and Coffin Company, were organized over the next few decades. New companies came, some failed, and others were bought out and merged into large corporations. Before too many years had passed, Lenoir and Caldwell County were known as the "Furniture Center of the South."

New businesses led to an influx of capital, and in 1894, the Bank of Lenoir was organized. This was followed by Commercial Bank in 1900 and the Bank of Granite in 1906. Another railroad penetrated Caldwell County in 1911. William J. Grandin from Pennsylvania purchased 60,000 acres of timber in Caldwell, Wilkes, and Watauga Counties. Grandin's plan was to harvest the timber and to extend his railroad, the Watauga and Yadkin River, all the way to Boone. A new mill town, named Grandin, was established, and the primeval forest of Caldwell disappeared at an alarming rate. The narrow-gauge Chester and Lenoir Railroad was reorganized in 1910, standard gauge line was laid, and the railroad was renamed the Carolina and Northwestern (C&NW).

In July 1916, a flood devastated much of Caldwell and surrounding counties. Dams were broken, homes destroyed, businesses and churches ruined, and railroad trestles washed out. Some towns, like Mortimer and Rhodhiss, were seriously damaged. An even further drain on the local economy occurred with the advent of "The Great War." Hundreds of Caldwell County men answered their country's call and joined the service.

Returning servicemen infused new life into the area, and the furniture industry continued to grow. Education was becoming more important to many across the state, and numerous one- and two-room schools across the county were consolidated into larger, better-staffed and equipped institutions. One educational loss was that of the Davenport College. The school was founded in Lenoir in 1855 as the Davenport Female Academy. In 1893, boys were admitted, and in 1915, the name was changed to Davenport College. In 1933, the school encountered difficulties and was closed and consolidated with the Greensboro College. The buildings became the property of the Lenoir School system.

One of the returning World War I veterans was James C. Harper. Harper was involved in the recently formed band of the Dysart-Kendall Post No. 29 of the American Legion in Lenoir. The members of the post band in 1924 gave their instruments to the Lenoir High School to form a band, one of the first in the state. The Lenoir High School band went on to become world famous, playing for governors and presidents and winning national championships. In 1977, the Lenoir High School was closed.

Other events followed, including another world war, depressions, and times of economic prosperity. Each event brought its own unique challenges as Caldwell County citizens rallied to support each other and the country at large during World War II and looked to the future with hope and enthusiasm as new businesses and educational endeavors flourished. In 1971, Caldwell Community College was established, providing college courses and vocational training for students of all ages.

In 1991, the last remaining building of the old Davenport College was loaned to the Caldwell County Historical Society to be used as a county museum. The old building today houses numerous artifacts from the different time periods of the county's history, from the frontier days to the men and women who have served their country, to railroads and the famed Lenoir High School Band. The Caldwell Heritage Museum is also a wonderful repository for hundreds of photographs, many of which illustrate this volume, photographs that tell of the history of Caldwell County.

One

COMMUNITY AND CHURCH

In January 1943, Lena Harmon and Vance Harmon joined Rev. Robert Shore in the cold waters of Bailey's Creek to be baptized. Although many churches have installed indoor, heated baptisteries in their sanctuaries, a few churches in Caldwell and other surrounding counties still practice the sacred ordinance of baptism in local creeks and rivers. These churches often have specific locations that they have used for generations. (Greene.)

The Johns River was an early recreational area. A successful dance hall entertained patrons until its destruction in the 1940 flood. Boating, fishing, and swimming were all popular activities, as seen here, with a well-dressed boating party enjoying the pleasant scenery while punting downstream. The river continues to attract visitors and local residents today. (Caldwell.)

Caldwell County's American Legion Post was organized in 1919 as Post 29. The first commander was James T. Pritchett. In 1921, the post was renamed the Dysart-Kendall Post to honor Pvt. Charles E. Dysart and Cpl. J. E. Kendall, two Caldwell County soldiers who had been killed in action in June 1918. The legion met in various sites around the county until construction of this fine facility, dedicated July 23, 1943. (Caldwell.)

The community of Grandin was begun by W. J. Grandin of Pennsylvania, who came to the area in 1912 to survey a possible railroad route. Like many other railroad owners, Grandin was heavily involved in the timber business and planned a spur to bring timber to Grandin from other areas. The town included a boarding house and homes for the workmen, and soon the railroad was running. However, the floods in 1916 and 1918 caused considerable damage. (Hsu.)

On July 5, 1845, citizens of Caldwell County gathered and decided to build a Methodist church in Lenoir. Building committee members included some of the most prominent members of the community, such as James Harper, Peter Ballew, Noah Spainhour, George Conley, N. A. Powell, J. H. Moore, and Azor Shell. In 1917, additional property was purchased for the First Methodist Church, and the current building, pictured in this postcard, was constructed. (Caldwell.)

Taken *c.* 1948, this photograph shows the members of Smith Memorial United Methodist Church, located in the Lower Creek Township. This church was organized in 1876 in a brush arbor on Stonewall Street, with the Rev. Bob Smith as pastor. The church was originally called the Smith Chapel Methodist Episcopal Church. The structure in this photograph was built in 1905. (Caldwell.)

This *c.* 1922 photograph, looking east up West Avenue, is the first known aerial view of Lenoir. A little over a decade later, according to a local newspaper, Lenoir had "8 department stores, 2 variety stores, 32 grocery stores, 2 jewelry stores, 5 hardware and furniture stores, 6 cafes, 2 hotels, 3 banks, 2 building and loans, 3 picture shows, 4 drug stores, 15 filling stations, 3 five and ten stores, 1 stationery store . . . and 10 insurance representatives." (Caldwell.)

Named for John H. Collett, the town of Collettsville gained its post office in 1837. Incorporation followed in 1897. Collettsville's economy was based around numerous sawmills. The lumber was floated down the river or brought in on trains, including the Chester and Lenoir Railroad, which later became the Carolina and Northwestern Railroad. The floods of 1916 and 1940 seriously damaged portions of the community and devastated the railroads. (Caldwell.)

Tabernacle Adventist Christian Church was first organized as the Tabernacle Church of Christ in 1876, under the leadership of George Durham Sherrill. A Caldwell County native, Sherrill enlisted in the Confederate army during the Civil War and was a prisoner of war at Hart's Island, where he began ministering as a chaplain to his fellow prisoners. The original congregation had 29 members and a small wooden building that evolved into this brick-fronted structure by 1945. (Caldwell.)

Members of the Baird family were among the original settlers of the Granite Falls area. The area takes its name from falls or shoals on Gunpowder Creek. A post office was established in the area in 1797. In the past 200 years, many businesses have prospered in the area, from Andrew Baird's forge in the late 1700s, to Keever's store, Moore Brothers, Mrs. Walter Russell's hat store, Hickman's Hardware, and the Kiser-Cline store. This photograph was taken *c.* 1915 (Caldwell.)

Located in the Patterson Township in Happy Valley, the home pictured here was known as Holly Lodge. It was constructed for Collett Leventhorpe, an English-born Confederate general. Leventhorpe moved to the area following the Civil War, and he and his wife, Louisa Bryan, divided their time between Holly Lodge, Watauga County to the north, New York, and London. The original Holly Lodge was destroyed by fire in May 1964. (Caldwell.)

The storage of ice prior to refrigeration was always a challenge. During the winter, when streams and ponds froze over, ice was carved out in huge blocks and taken to homes, where it was stored in deep pits, packed in sawdust. The ice would keep for months. The Beall Ice Pond, located between Broadway and Beall Streets in Lenoir, provided locals with ice for many generations. (Caldwell.)

Kings Creek Baptist Church was organized in 1779 and moved to its present location in 1860. The two doors at the front of this building harken back to an era when men entered and sat on one side of the building, while the ladies entered another door and sat on the other side. A new building was constructed between 1973 and 1975. (Caldwell.)

The First Presbyterian Church of Lenoir was the county's first Presbyterian church at its founding in 1852. The first building was a log structure that was also used by other congregations. In 1859, the church built its own building and by 1857 had secured its first full-time pastor, Jesse Rankin. In 1904, a new brick building was completed, and the present brick, Colonial-style building was dedicated in 1970. The church cemetery is pictured here. (Hardy.)

Berea Advent Christian Church, shown here about 1930, was established in the 1870s in Collettsville. Rev. John A. Cargile of Stephenson, Alabama, was the first pastor. The present building was constructed in the 1930s, following the flood of 1916 that washed the old church building, located near John's River, from its foundation. (Greene.)

Sometime between 1814 and 1840, George Powell constructed Red Grange, better known as the Keyhole House. Believing that evil spirits burned his first house, Powell designed the home with a keyhole shape cut out near the roof to allow witches and other unfriendly beings to escape. The house fell into disrepair and was torn down in the early 1970s for construction of the Trinity United Methodist Church Sanctuary. The keyhole was preserved as part of the church's sign. (Caldwell.)

Prior to the Civil War, both Presbyterian and Methodist congregations used the Fairfield community building, which was built by James Harper. Both congregations later built their own buildings, and the Fairfield Church is no longer standing, but its cemetery remains. Buried here is Ephraim Clayton Jr., son of renowned builder Ephraim Clayton, who was in the area working on public buildings at the time of his son's death. (Hardy.)

This image of the community of Patterson includes the post office, mill, and Smith Store. Patterson was formed around the successful cotton mill, which was founded by Gen. Samuel F. Patterson in 1850. The once-thriving community had a mayor and commissioners, but it is now unincorporated. The area is home to the Patterson Boarding School. (Caldwell.)

Deacons and elders of the Old Evangelical Reformed Church who had their photograph taken in the sanctuary are, from left to right, (first row) Earl Abernathy, Paul Hedrick, George Rabb, K. A. Link, and John Ingle; (second row) Fred Boyd, Dennis Rabb, John Bost, Dr. ? Rowe, John Brookshire, Harlan Deal, and Bob Hedrick; (third row) Perry Carpenter, Verne Blackwelder, Carroll Rabb, Joe Sullivan, Clyde Hedrick, and Roy Shoaf. (Caldwell.)

The town of Mortimer sprang up almost overnight. Located in the northern section of Caldwell County, Mortimer was a company town for the Ritter Lumber Company and was incorporated in 1907. Not only were there over 100 houses and the lumber company buildings, but also two churches, a school, a hotel, a company store, and a blacksmith shop. The 1940 flood destroyed most of the town. (Caldwell.)

Buffalo Cove Baptist Church was established May 8, 1851, by 13 people. The first pastor was Burton Bradley, and pastors served the church for one year only. The first building was likely a log structure, the second was built between 1895 and 1896, and the third building, seen here, was built between 1952 and 1953. In 1999, the church created a community park on its property. (Caldwell.)

The Chapel of Rest, on land belonging to the Patterson School, was originally constructed in 1889. A fire destroyed the structure in 1917, but rebuilding took place the following year. The Chapel of Rest is no longer used as a place for regular worship, but many special events take place there. A cemetery behind the chapel predates the structure. (Caldwell.)

Hillside Cottage was constructed in 1843 by James Harper as a home for Emma J. Baker, her widowed mother, and two younger sisters. Baker came to Lenoir to teach at Montrose Academy. The house was later occupied by the Rev. Jesse Rankin family and the Rev. John Watts and was purchased by Hugh C. Hamilton in 1862. The property has passed through many other hands in the past 100 years and has recently been restored. (Hardy.)

St. James Episcopal Church was constituted on May 24, 1849. The building, enclosed by an iron fence, was completed two years later. During the last days of the Civil War, the church grounds were pressed into service as a prison, holding Confederates captured during Gen. George Stoneman's raid. The church was extensively remodeled in 1962, but it still occupies its place on Main Street and College Avenue. (Caldwell.)

Johannes A. Oertel was born in Furth, Bavaria, in 1823, and came to the United States in 1848. He engraved banknotes from 1852 until 1857, and in 1867, he was ordained as an Episcopal deacon and then as a priest in 1871. He lived in Lenoir from 1869 until 1876. During this time, he painted the altar at St. James Church. At various times, he lived in Morganton; Washington, D.C.; Sewanee, Tennessee; and St. Louis, Missouri. (Caldwell.)

21

Union Baptist Church was organized June 2, 1814, when the county was still Burke County. The first pastor was William Dotson. The first building was built of pine logs and was used until 1875, when the congregation built a larger, one-room structure. In 1940, plans were begun for the current building, seen here. The structure was dedicated Easter Sunday, 1942. A parsonage and educational building were added in the 1950s, and a baptistery was added in 1967. (McRee.)

Mariah's Chapel was established in the mid-1800s as a joint meeting place for both the Methodists and Episcopalians in the Yadkin Valley Township area. It was named "Mariah" in honor of Martha Maria Earnest, the daughter of David and Elizabeth Eveline Jones Earnest. Lewis Shuford was Sunday school superintendent for over 50 years. (Hsu.)

Hudson started out as Hudsonville in the 1880s, but by 1889, the "ville" had been dropped due to confusion with the post office in Hendersonville. Hudson began as a logging camp, with sawmills devouring the wooded hillsides. The arrival of the railroad jump-started the local economy. When the timber ran out, businesses set up shop, such as the Hudson Cotton Mill in 1904. This is an early view of the downtown area. (Caldwell.)

At one time, Patterson was a thriving community, replete with a mayor and town commissioners. The Patterson Cotton Mill provided much of the impetus behind the community's success. The Mill was started by Samuel Patterson, burned by Stoneman's Raiders during the Civil War, and then rebuilt. The mill was later reorganized as the Gwyn-Harper Manufacturing Company. (Caldwell.)

Some of the first settlers to arrive in what would become Caldwell County came to an area called Happy Valley. The Lenoirs settled in the area in the late 1700s, followed by the Joneses, Pattersons, and others. Happy Valley was a fertile region, and this photograph, taken c. 1870, shows the area under cultivation. (Caldwell.)

Palmyra was the home of Samuel Ledgerwood Patterson and his wife, Mary S. Senseman of Salem. Patterson inherited the estate upon the death of his father, Gen. Samuel Finley Patterson, in 1874. When Patterson died in 1908, his property was converted into an industrial and agricultural school, as he had wished. The beautiful house, pictured here, was used as a dormitory, but it burned in 1922. (Patterson.)

This early-20th-century Bible convention was attended by Finley Patterson Coffey (standing, far left), a charter member of the First Baptist Church of Lenoir. Patterson was born in 1848 and died in 1937. It is also interesting to note that a woman and little girl (center) are at the conference, along with an African American man (left), who is holding a bell. (Throneburg.)

First known as the Tucker family farm, the area around present-day Lenoir was settled around 1765. In 1775, Fort Grider was constructed to protect settlers against Native American attacks. In 1841, when the county was created, Tucker's Barn was chosen to be the new county seat and named in honor of Gen. William Lenoir. This view, with mule- and oxen-drawn wagons, was taken after the erection of the Confederate monument in 1910. (Caldwell.)

This image, taken between 1910 and 1920, captures the crops of James Willis George in the foreground. In the background, a railroad trestle for the Carolina and Northwestern Railroad is clearly visible. The George property, on which the trestle stood, is off Harrisburg Road, and the Bernhardt Central Lumber Yard stands there today. (Caldwell.)

The Deal Farm, pictured here, was the home place of the Deal family. The first of the Deals in the region was William Deal, who came to Mecklenburg County in 1767. His grandson, William Deal III, was a very successful Caldwell County farmer and businessman who, at the age of 63, left this thriving farm to serve in the North Carolina Home Guard during the Civil War. Six of his sons were also Civil War soldiers. (McRee.)

Two

EDUCATION

In 1938, the *Caldwell Photo News* reported that there were 6,455 students enrolled in Caldwell County schools. Most of them were educated in schoolrooms like the one above, at the White Springs School, pictured here in the early 1930s. (Caldwell.)

The Collettsville High School girls' basketball team for 1926 was coached by Mr. McNeely. Members pictured from left to right are (first row) Wilma Moore, Edna Houck, Margaret Glass, Lucy Franklin, and Hortense Rader; (second row) Coach McNeely, Alma Moore, Bernice Clark, Bessie Rader, Bessie Grisette, Daisy Spenser, and Minnie Glass. (Beane.)

From 1924 until Lenoir High School closed in 1977, the Lenoir High School band performed for audiences throughout the nation. The band appeared in motion pictures, played on the radio, and made numerous recordings. They also won countless awards, dominating much larger schools across the state. (Caldwell.)

Members of the Davenport School art class in this image are, from left to right, (first row) Susie Clarke Triplett, Eva Goforth, and Rose Earnhardt; (second row) Alice Conley, Amanda Clarke (teacher), Connor Sherrill, Alice Powell, Mary L. Pulliam, Florence Boyd, and Mattie Baker; (third row) Alice Woodliff, Eolens Hailey, Edith Kinkaid, Pearl Clarke, and Kate Wedby. (Caldwell.)

A school has been located in Happy Valley since before the Civil War. This brick structure was constructed in 1925, and classes were held for the first time in January 1926. Talmadge Smith was the principal, and Beatrice Watts, Coleen Wall, H. B. Steele, and Mary L. Dobbins were teachers. The school gained accreditation with the state in 1933. (Caldwell.)

Gamewell Graded School teachers from the class of 1937 are, from left to right, (first row) Rena Stroup, Hazel Beard, Mae Courtney, and Ruth Black; (second row) Reese Corpening, Dora Anderson, Lottie Suddreth, Mrs. George Tuttle, Mrs. Ben Hood, Lucille Deal, and Carolyn Suddreth. (Thorneburg.)

In 1929, room one of the Baton School had this image taken. Included here are, from left to right, (first row) Virginia Bell Hollar, Louise McCall, Wilda Smith, Nina Mae Smith, Margaret Smith, Ruby Prestwood, Alene Smith, Barbara Setzer, and Celeste McCall; (second row) Murial Annas, Gwyn Setzer, Walter Elrod, Coy Setzer, Marshall Shell, Harold Smith, Vern Craig, Murphy Smith, Perry Duncan, Tom Price, Hugh Price, Alvin Brooks, J. D. Smith, and Elizabeth Joplin Crouch (teacher); (third row) Burl Smith, Pearl McCall, Leona McCall, ? Spann, Violet Hice, Emily Beane, Effie Craig, Sadie Lingerfelt, and Frank Hood; (fourth row) Arnold Craig, Thad Smith, Jay Beane, Hickman Crotts, ? Elrod, Paul Smith, Harley Bolick, Herbert Smith, unidentified, Shorty Bolick, and Arnold Bolick. (Hawkins.)

The one-room Shady Grove School was located on Lower Draco Road on property donated by Sion Oxford. A few of the teachers who taught at this school before it was consolidated with Oak Hill were Lina Deal, Tom Roberts, Lucille Deal, Mae Tolbert, Mildred Parlier, Jane Reid, Robert Austin, Addie Brown, Rose Reid, and Pansy Roberts. (Caldwell.)

Lenoir High School boys' basketball team for 1933 consisted of, from left to right, (first row) Paul Grist (manager), J. Oakley, Mack Cook, Willard Church, Joe Rabb, and Ray Kirby; (second row) Clarence Holden, Bill Buys, Paul Oakley, Colon Price, George Petrie, and Coach Andrew Radar. (Caldwell.)

Cottrell Hill School was founded in 1876. Several years later, the school gained a new building, then two teachers and two rooms. This photograph of the student body of the Cottrell Hill School was taken on October 19, 1933. About 1936, Cottrell Hill was consolidated with Kings Creek School. (Caldwell.)

Lenoir Grade School was founded in 1904 and located on North Main Street. An early newspaper stated the school "had 10 recitation rooms, plenty of hall space on the first and second floors, a reception room, the superintendent's private apartment, and a large auditorium." The auditorium was "furnished with opera chairs on the first floor and with raised seats on the second." There was also "water, hot air heat, and gasoline lighting." (Caldwell.)

Pictured here from left to right are members of the 1925 freshman class of Lenoir High School arrayed on the steps of the school: (first row) Cecil Benfield, Dick Herman, Hal Hayes, Rufus Kinkaid, Arthur Allen, Curtis Deitz, James Caudle, Ted Broyhill, John Tipton, Paul Hedrick, Paul Chester, and ? Miller; (second row) Helen Winkler, Mary Torrence, Mazie Blaylock, Evelyn Caudle, Hazel Hollifield, Pauline Robbins, Texie Craig, Charlotte Peeler, and Hazel Beard; (third row) Grace Seehorn, Pansy Angley, Gerald Gregg, Nannie Pipes, May Angley, Nealie Foster, Asilee Powell, Mabel Klutz, Marie Price, Mary Smith, Elizabeth Allen, unidentified, Josephine Courtney, unidentified, Virgie Cook, Bonnie Bean, ? Holloway, Ruth Black, unidentified, Flora Lou Wilson, Flossie Pulliam, Bettie Neal Triplett, and George Norris; (fourth row) Ben Eller, unidentified, John Bingham, Bill Triplett, Tom Ell Seehorn, Edward Dula, David Sprinkle, Louis Watson, Edward Hamby, and Fred Melton. (Caldwell.)

The chemistry class at Happy Valley School in 1949 included, from left to right, (first row) Bonnie Hagaman, Viola Bolick, Shirley Winkler, Alma Bolick, and Dorsie Bolick; (second row) Fred Bryant, Betty Sue Greene, and Melba Storie Hartley; (third row) Bill Isaacs and Edwin Greene. The high school portion of the Happy Valley School was consolidated with high schools from Kings Creek and Oak Hill to form the Hibriten High School in 1966. (Greene.)

This view of the interior of the third-grade school room at King's Creek School was taken in the early 1930s. The school was first started as the Kings Creek Academy in 1894 by the Reverend W. R. Beach and his wife. The school was later turned into a free public school. (Caldwell.)

In the fall of 1909, the Oak Hill High School was formed, consolidating the smaller schools of Cedar Valley, Union, Throneburg, Shady Grove, and Draco. The only rural high school in this part of the state, the original school only had three rooms. In this image, several of the school's later buildings are visible, including the "teacherage" on the right. The school was combined with King's Creek and Happy Valley in 1966, forming Hibriten School. (McRee.)

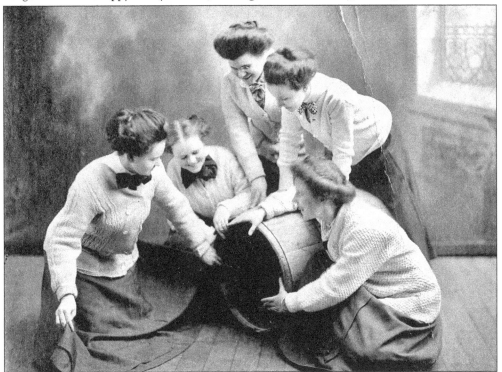

The members of the Davenport School Rabbit Club posed for this picture shortly before 1920, but the rabbit seems reluctant to make an appearance. The students, from left to right, are Jewel Wombler, Lizzie Wreen, Lelia Hinder, May Wreen, and Hazel McAdams. (Caldwell.)

The Bailey Camp School students in this 1934 image are, from left to right, (first row) Hazel Bolick, Lea Hamlet, Elsie Harmon, Emma Bolick, Edna Harmon, Eula Hamlet, Opal Bolick, and Carrie Harmon; (second row) Warren Ford, Clell Bolick, Clarence Ford, Ellis Harmon, Vance Harmon, George Harmon, Vonley Ford, and Claude Harmon; (third row) Gordon Bolick, Daisy Teague, Ada Bolick, Ira Ford, John Harmon, and Clyde Teague; (fourth row) Doyle Bolick, Johnny Ford, Bill Hamlet, William Ford, Mary Hamlet, Ruth Bolick, and Fay Hamlet. (Greene.)

Here the members of the graduating class of 1941 from Hudson High School pose in front of one of the old Davenport College buildings. Davenport College closed in 1933, and Hudson High School, which operated from 1881 until 1977, used one of its buildings after losing its own in a fire. Only one of the buildings from Davenport College survives, and it is used today as the Caldwell Heritage Museum. (Caldwell.)

The school in Rhodhiss, pictured here in the early 1930s, began in 1900 as a school for the children of the men building the mill. By 1903, a free public school had been started in Rhodhiss. In 1907, the students were meeting in a two-story structure. By 1941, the school had 236 scholars and 7 teachers. (Caldwell.)

Davenport Junior Band
Madeline G. Herman, Director

State Contest, Greensboro
1960 - Superior

The Davenport School started as Central Elementary School, which moved onto the old Davenport College campus in 1947. The school first gained accreditation in 1967. The Davenport Junior Band, pictured here after obtaining a "superior" rating at a state contest in Greensboro in 1960, practiced in the old college dining hall, which had been converted into an auditorium, until the late 1970s. Pictured here with the band is Madeline G. Herman, director. (Caldwell.)

This image captures the Puett Hill School third- and fourth-grade classes in 1922. The school was located in Collettsville and was the first school in the community when it was established in 1867. The original building was made of log and had a six-foot fireplace to warm students when drafts came through the logs. Pictured from left to right are (first row) Orren Puett; (second row) Coyt Estes, Fred Spencer, Fate Puett, Watt Estes, Jonas Johnson, Joe Leonard, and Richard Estes; (third row) Gladys Spencer, Shirley Moore, Vivian Grisette, unidentified, Era Puett, Margaret Webb, Annie Greene, Marie Estes, and unidentified; (fourth row) Julia Spencer, Hortense Rader, Jessie Estes, Vernie Tolbert, Maggie Joe Estes, Della Mae Setzer, Mary Estes, Alma Bowman, Mertie Bowman, and Hattie Estes (teacher); (fifth row) Miss ? Davis (teacher), Ulysses Grisette, Wayne Moore, Rube Leonard, Tommy Moore, Ben Leonard, Jay Spencer, Dave Rader, Cecil Clark, and Gene Rader. (Beane.)

The Lenoir High School Band poses here in October 1936 in front of one of their red transport buses. The band had competed in the 1933 state music contest, placing first or second in 17 of the 20 categories. Three years after this photograph was taken, the band traveled to New York in the same bus to participate in the New York World's Fair. (Caldwell.)

Pearl Thompson and Sylvester Cobb were teachers at the Bailey Camp School prior to 1923. Neither Thompson nor Cobb were from Caldwell County, but they came from outside the area to help educate local children. While many local schools did have teachers that came from the area, importing teachers was not an uncommon practice. (Greene.)

Gamewell School teachers for 1931–1932 were, from left to right, (first row) Mae Courtney, Nell Throneburg, and Lottie Suddreth; (second row) Dora Anderson, ? Sherrill, Mrs. George Tuttle, Mrs. Ben Hood, and Mrs. Estelle Link. It is interesting to note that all of the married teachers are older ladies, most likely with grown children. Recently married ladies or those with young children were usually not allowed to be teachers. (Throneburg.)

Buffalo Cove School students pictured from left to right are (first row) Myrtle Robbins, Ester Watson, Ruby Lee Cottrell, Sergie Coffey, Cara Mae Cottrell, Pauline Cottrell, Eunice Adams, Martha Day, unidentified, and Nina Todd; (second row) Billy Taylor, Jonathan Robbins, Keyner Bell, Maynard Robbins, Ernest Watson, Eugene Coffey, Eugene Howard, Keyna Hawkins, and Adair Hawkins; (third row) Darman Cottrell, Rodney Miller, Luther Adams, Granville Robbins, Henry Coffey, Clarence Cottrell, and Dennis Coffey; (fourth row includes) Bertie Watson, ? Barnett, Faye Cottrell, Georgia Robbins, and Flossie Robbins. (Hawkins.)

Miller Hill High School was in existence by 1913. Mary Seehorn and Stella McQuery were two of the school's early teachers. Miller High School was consolidated with the Whitnel School in 1933 and appears abandoned in this mid-1930s photograph. (Caldwell.)

The Lenoir High School girls' basketball team for 1937–1938 stands outside the school. The team included Jewel Hall Winkler (second from left on first row), Dot Winkler Ludwig (third from left on second row), Maude Winkler Belko (fifth from left on second row), and Mary Elma Winkler Baskervill (sixth from left on second row). (Winkler.)

Mount Herman School students pictured in December 1931 were, from left to right, (first row) Ruth Cobb, Blanche West, Hannah West, Pauline Williams, Colene Cobb, Faye Tolbert, Ivora Bumgarner, Ruby Smith, Mildred Haas, Bernice Haas, and Helen Roberts; (second row) Leonard Sullivan, Glenn Williams, Maynard Tolbert, Erwin Williams, Bruce Haas, Troy Smith, Bert Cline, Gene Tolbert, Ernest Tolbert, and Marvin Haas; (third row includes) Janey Chester, Pansy Tolbert, Virgie Cobb, Mable Smith, Bernice Sullivan, Jewel Hart, and Miss Anderson; (fourth row) Clem Sullivan, Fred Cobb, Weyburn Smith, Harvey Bollinger, Marjorie Hart, Ned West, and Beckley Haas. (Clark.)

Freedman School was established in 1904 as an elementary school for African American students. A four-room building was constructed in 1926. The new building, shown in this photograph taken in 1926, housed grades one through seven and also contained a chapel. The building also later housed the Freedman High School, created in 1932. The school system was integrated in 1967, and the school became the William Lenoir Middle School. (Caldwell.)

42

The members of the 1951–1952 fourth-grade class of Mrs. Dorothy Haymaker at Gamewell Elementary were, from left to right, (first row includes) Peggy Jones, Judy Triplett, Della Reichard, Edwina Bylery, Modine Crump, Billie Jean Powell, Lucy Moore, Peggy Sue Conley, Patsy Gilbert, and Diane Galzebrook; (second row) Doris Whisnant, Mary Ann Golds, Geneva Messer, Mae Bell Smith, Earline Bryant, Asalee Beaver, Doris Small, Mary Jo Hamby, and Louise Shantly; (third row) Ray Melton, Ralph Parsons, Grady Carswell, Ted Walker, Bill Jones, Reginald Cinhaneh, Johnny Franklin, Terry Reynolds, Bob Melton, Edward Byrd, Doug McDonald, and Don Chandler. (Triplett.)

Members of an early Lenoir High School girls' basketball team were, from left to right, (first row) Lila Holhouser, Peg Bradford, ? Ballew, Grace Haas, Helen Ludwig, and Mary Emma Crews; (second row) Margaret Beech (manager), Vivian Huntley, Margaret Lacky, Olen Barlow, Lib Dula, Mary Douglass McCully, Helen Huntley, and Coach Mary Moore. (Caldwell.)

These Gamewell seventh-grade students photographed in 1934 are, from left to right, (first row) Lelia T. Hoover, Ruth Clay, Faye Rodes, Ruth Beard, unidentified, Emogene White, Jewel Anderson, Josephine Houck, and Lucille Miller; (second row) Javan Kinkaid, Woody Suddreth, Henry Query, James Suddreth, Fritz Arney, James Helton, ? Parson, unidentified, and Howard Miller; (third row) Lois Sharpe, Faye Anderson, Edna Jenkins, Margaret ?, Rachel Craig, Margaret Moore, ? Baker, and Lizzie McGoor; (fourth row) Margaret Anderson, Marvin Suddreth, unidentified, Paul Kinkaid, Claude Arney, Clyde Watson, Wade Suddreth, and Janie Mash. (Throneburg.)

In this 1950s image, students at the Patterson School stand around the flagpole in front of the Palmyra administration building. The original Palmyra was the home of Patterson School founder Samuel Ledgerwood Patterson and was used as a student dormitory until it burned in 1922. The new building was constructed in 1927. (Patterson.)

The very first Lenoir High School band was formed in 1924. The first band uniforms, pictured here being worn by the drum majors, consisted of a cape, coat, white shirt, tie, and trousers. The "Lenoir High School Band" logo appears on the chimes, but the flag in the background is the Bearcats flag. (Caldwell.)

The "Old Academy," also known as the Douglass Academy, was one of the first schools for African Americans in Caldwell County. The school sat where Belleview Cemetery is now located, on East Finley Avenue. Margaret Dula is in the center of this 1916 photograph, holding her hat. (Caldwell.)

Davenport Female College was first opened in July 1858 and had 56 students enrolled in 1859. The first board of trustees consisted of James C. Harper, Edmund Jones, Nelson Powell, Sidney P. Dula, and Azor Shell. Sponsored by the Methodist Episcopal Church South, the college included the handsome building captured in this pre-1877 photograph. The structure cost 10,000 to build, and the cupola was equipped with telescopes for astronomy classes. The college was a successful educational enterprise at the time of the February 15, 1877, fire that was caused by chimney sparks. The main building and other college buildings were burned to the ground in a matter of hours. The school recovered from the fire and in 1893 began admitting male students. Accordingly, in 1915, the name was changed to Davenport College. The college continued educating students until its consolidation with Greensboro College. Several buildings were later used by the school system, and one of the fine buildings currently houses the Caldwell Heritage Museum. (Caldwell.)

Three

FRIENDS AND FAMILY

Members of the Dock Clarke family of Collettsville, shown in 1928, are, from left to right, (first row) Ernestine Clarke, Dock Clarke, Hazel Clarke, Rachel Coffey Clarke, Helen Clarke, Dora Clarke, and Tony Clarke; (second row) Fray Clarke, Lonnie Clarke, Frances Clarke, Jean Clarke, Bernice Clarke, Dock Clarke Jr., and Bryant Clarke. (Beane.)

Anne Kent was the daughter of Robert and Zella Kent and was born in Lenoir in 1919. She was a graduate of Hudson High School and the Lenoir Business College. She married Malcolm Vance Hickman, right, and became a sales representative for the Penn Central Railroad. Later she was vice chairman of the North Carolina Republican Party and organized the North Carolina Federation of Republican Women. She died in 2004. (Hsu.)

Granite Falls native Sara E. Payne Hayden joined the army as a Women's Airforce Service Pilot (WASP) in 1944, only one of 1,830 successful candidates out of the 25,000 who applied. The WASP members towed targets across the sky for target practice and simulated bombing runs, among other duties. Hayden later served as a recruiter and commercial pilot, and she helped found an organization for former WASPs in the 1960s. (Caldwell.)

These two lovely ladies are Laura Pulliam (left) and Brenda Holloway (Stallings). At the age of 14, Laura Pulliam was Miss Lenoir in 1933. The event was Lenoir's first beauty pageant and was sponsored by the American Legion Auxiliary. Brenda Holloway became "Miss North Carolina Teen-ager" for 1974–1975 and was the fifth runner-up in the national competition held in Hawaii. (Dula and Holloway.)

This photograph, taken by Teague Studios in Lenoir, chronicles the July 15, 1915, wedding of Edward Lee Steele and Willie Anson Tuttle. The wedding party included, from left to right, Imogene Tuttle Hamby (bride's sister), Sarah Steele (groom's mother), John Steele (groom's father), Edward Lee Steele, Willie Anson Tuttle, Bertha Mason Tuttle (bride's sister), and ? Steele (groom's sister). The wedding was held at the groom's family home on Prospect Street in Lenior. (George.)

Born in Virginia, William Lenoir migrated with his family to North Carolina in 1759. By 1776, he was living in the Yadkin River Valley when the American Revolution began. Lenoir actively supported the patriots during the war and, in 1780, commanded a company during the Battle of King's Mountain, in which he was wounded. The patriot victory at King's Mountain changed the course of the war. Following American independence, Lenoir purchased property in present-day Caldwell County and, by 1791, was living in a new home called Fort Defiance. Lenoir continued to be active in local and state affairs. He was at different times county register, county surveyor, chairman of the county court, clerk of the superior court for Wilkes County, major general in the state militia, state representative, and state senator, serving as speaker of the state senate for five years. General Lenoir died in 1839, at the age of 88, and is buried in the family cemetery at Fort Defiance. (Caldwell.)

Born in 1860, Samuel Moses Larkin Jones retired from teaching in public schools in Caldwell County in 1943. Jones taught in the Harpertown and Warrior communities. He was the son of Horace and Leatha Jones, a graduate of Bennett College in Greensboro, and a member of the Odd Fellows. Jones died in 1945. (Caldwell.)

"Granny Deal" (Sarah Catharine McCall Deal) was born in 1850. She had five brothers who served as soldiers during the Civil War, all of whom returned home, and she recalled knitting socks and making clothing during the war years. Granny Deal, who loved to read, lived until October 1955, dying six weeks before her 105th birthday. (Caldwell.)

The Corley family of Lizard Ridge poses in a typical fashion for early portrait photography. A sheet, quilt, or photographer's backdrop was hung outdoors, often, as here, on a building. Usually the edges of the image would be cropped so that it appeared as though the subjects were seated in a studio, rather than in their yards. From left to right are J. E. Corley, Ed Corley, Harriett Corley, and George Corley. (Corley.)

The children of Thomas P. and Mary Ann (German) Winkler are pictured from left to right: Thomas Lloyd Winkler (1905–1979), Annie Thomasie Winkler Jones (1903–1984), Lucille Nannie Winkler (1900–1974), Albert (Ab) Ross Winkler (1897–1973), Lillie Lee Winkler West (1893–1973), Florence Winkler Sharpe (1891–1971), and Fannie Bell Winkler Herman (1889–1962). (Winkler.)

Members of the Cicero Levi Harmon family pictured are, from left to right, (first row) Levi Harmon, Alex Harmon, Rufus Harmon, Eli Harmon, and Philo Harmon; (second row) Eli Bolick with Fred Bolick, Callie Harmon Bolick with Ralph Lee Bolick, Samantha Harmon Greene with Rinda Greene, Cicero Levi Harmon, Laura Ann Moore Harmon with Toy Harmon Greene, and Julia Ann Harmon Curtis; (third row) Pumroy Harmon, Rose Harmon Curtis, Dora Harmon Greene, Dock Greene, Jesse Wilson, Lelia Harmon Wilson, Lola Harmon Wilson, and possibly Elizabeth Estes Greene. (Greene.)

Willis G. Haymaker Jr., pictured here standing watch on board the USS *Missouri*, his U.S. Navy training vessel, moved with his parents to Caldwell County from Indiana in 1931. His parents were Willis and Dorothy Taylor Haymaker. Willis G. Haymaker Sr. served as crusade director for the Billy Graham Evangelistic Association from 1949 until 1969. (Caldwell.)

Caldwell County has sent several of its local baseball players to play in the major leagues. John Allen (top left), a Lenoir native, played for the New York Yankees (1932–1935), the Cleveland Indians (1936–1940), the St. Louis Browns (1941), the Brooklyn Dodgers (1941–1943), and the New York Giants (1943–1944). He played on the World Series–winning Yankees in 1932. Albert "Rube" Walker (top right) of Lenoir was a catcher and played for the Chicago Cubs (1948–1951), the Brooklyn Dodgers (1951–1957), and the Los Angeles Dodgers (1958). The Dodgers went to the World Series in 1952, 1953, 1955, and 1956, taking the championship in 1955. Lenoir native Lindsey Deal (bottom left), an outfielder, played one season for the Brooklyn Dodgers (1939). Jack Curtis (bottom right), who was from Rhodhiss, pitched for the Chicago Cubs (1961–1962), the Milwaukee Braves (1963), and the Cleveland Indians (1963). (Caldwell.)

Members of the Estes family from the Globe section of Caldwell County are pictured from left to right: (first row) Belle Estes, Mary Estes Triplett (the only Caldwell County woman to serve as sheriff), Maude Estes Moore, and Helen Estes Phillips; (second row) Bertha Estes, Gordon Estes, Lank Estes, and Clara Estes Moore. (Beane.)

Carl Story was born in Lenoir in 1926 and learned to play fiddle at an early age. Pictured here with members of the Indian River Rangers, Story would later be better known as the "Father of Bluegrass Gospel Music." Story formed both the Lonesome Mountaineers and the Rambling Mountaineers in the 1930s. In 1942, Story fiddled for Bill Monroe and his Blue Grass Boys until 1943, when he was drafted. After World War II, Story re-formed the Rambling Mountaineers and played up until his death in 1995. (Caldwell.)

The three Houck sisters in this portrait are, from left to right, Clara Ann Houck Anderson, Bellona "Dink" Houck Anderson, and Florence Houck Coffey. After Clara's death, Bellona married her late sister's husband, James Alexander Anderson, and cared for her nieces and nephews as her own children, hence their identical maiden and married names. (Triplett.)

Born in Lenoir in 1942, Larry Smith was Caldwell County's most famous NASCAR driver. His debut was at the World 600 in 1971. In 1972, Smith was named NASCAR's first Rookie of the Year. Carling Black Label came on board as his sponsor for the 1973 season. At the Talladega 500 on August 12, 1973, Smith spun into the wall on lap 14 and suffered massive head trauma that led to his death. (LeFever.)

Lenoir's first mayor was Clinton A. Cilley. Born in New Hampshire in 1837, Cilley moved to Minnesota prior to the Civil War. He became captain of Company C, 2nd Minnesota Infantry, and won the Medal of Honor for bravery during the Battle of Chickamauga, Georgia. Cilley worked with the Freedman's Bureau after the war and moved to the Lenoir-Hickory area. Cilley married Emma Sophia Harper and became mayor of Lenoir in 1885; later he served as a judge. Cilley died in 1900. (Caldwell.)

Pictured from left to right are the Winkler brothers, Lawrence, Clarence, and Green. Lawrence River Winkler was born February 17, 1873, and died December 16, 1966. He married Rosa B. Turner. Clarence Columbus Winkler was born March 27, 1875, and died January 6, 1958. He married Kate Bean. Green Wilborn Winkler was born February 27, 1880, and died April 24, 1973. He married Ada Kincaid. (Winkler.)

Walter J. Lenoir, the son of Rufus Lenoir, was a leading civic leader and business executive. He was educated at the University of North Carolina and then returned to Caldwell County. In 1908, he became one of the founders of the Lenoir Hardware and Furniture Company, and for seven terms, he was mayor of Lenoir. Walter was married to Harriet Augusta Horton of Happy Valley. (Caldwell.)

These lawmen look ready for action with their drawn pistols. In fact, Sheriff John Smith (right) and the chief of police (left) are apparently preparing for a manhunt with the bloodhounds. Although bloodhounds have often been used to track escaped convicts and other fugitives from justice, their name actually comes from the fact that long ago in Europe, only aristocrats, "blooded" people, could own them. (Caldwell.)

James T. Broyhill was a native of Lenoir who served as an executive with Broyhill Furniture Industries before his successful entrance into politics. He represented the 9th and 10th Congressional Districts in the U.S. House of Representatives from 1963 until 1986. Thereafter he served as a senator from July 14, 1986, until November 4, 1986. He was a popular and involved leader who supported many Caldwell County projects, including the restoration of Fort Defiance, markers for the Overmountain Victory Trail, and other historical efforts. He remained active in civic and church duties throughout his political service. Broyhill was a graduate of the University of North Carolina at Chapel Hill and, in 1966, was awarded an honorary Doctor of Laws degree from Catawba College in Salisbury. Prior to his political career, he was the 1957 Lenoir Junior Chamber of Commerce's "Young Man of the Year." (Caldwell.)

Second Lt. Dudley F. Nelson Jr. of Lenoir was an F-86 Sabrejet pilot with the Air Force 4th Fighter Interceptor Wing during the Korean War. This photograph, dated June 18, 1953, documents Dudley's June 16 mission, in which he damaged a MIG-15 fighter over northwest Korea. It was his first "score" against a MIG. (Caldwell.)

The five Houck brothers in this early-20th-century image are, from left to right, (first row) George Houck and Edward Columbus "Tom" Houck; (second row) Elam "Son" Houck, Benedict "Dick" Houck, and Grover Houck. They were the sons of Robert Caldwell "Bob" Houck and Margaret Isabell "Bell" Hood whose farm was on Rocky Road, near the Bee Mountains. (Triplett.)

According to family legend, Joshua Hawkins of Rowan County fought at King's Mountain and was persuaded by General Lenoir to settle on Buffalo Creek. The Hawkins family cemetery is located on his original land grant. Joshua's great grandson is here pictured with his wife and family, including three of his own grandchildren, from left to right: Granville Hawkins, Susan Adeline Turnmire Hawkins, Sophia Turnmire Robbins, Lowery Hawkins, John L. Hawkins, Ida Hawkins, and Mollie Hawkins. (Hawkins.)

The four children of J. E. Broyhill and Satie Leona Hunt were, from left to right, James (Jim), Allene, Paul, and Bettie. J. E. Broyhill was an important civic, business, and church leader who served on the boards of the National Association of Manufacturers, C&NW Railway, and Wachovia Bank, among others. Several buildings, parks, grants, and foundations also bear the Broyhill name, legacy of the family's commitment to service. (Hsu.)

The Ford and Bolick families lived in the northern sections of Caldwell County. This early-20th-century photograph portrays the John Ford family, from left to right are Sarah, Ola, Pearl, Lizzie, Mary, Clarissa, Barbara (Bolick), Ethel, Johnny, William, John, and Darius Ford. (Greene.)

Samuel Ledgerwood Patterson was born March 8, 1850, in Happy Valley. A large landholder and proponent of agricultural science, Patterson was a county commissioner, state senator, and North Carolina Commissioner of Agriculture for four terms. In his will, he made provisions for his estate to become an industrial and agricultural school for boys. Upon his death in 1908, this wish was fulfilled with the formation of the Patterson School. (Patterson.)

John Harrison Gibson served in Company I of the 26th North Carolina Troops, known as the Caldwell Guards, during the Civil War. He and his two brothers were all wounded at Gettysburg. The 26th suffered more casualties than any other regiment at the battle. Here he is pictured with his second wife, Selenia Smith Gibson, with whom he had three children. (Gibson.)

In December 1943, these seven Caldwell County natives found themselves on the same island in the South Pacific. Pictured from left to right are (first row) John Crisp, from the Globe; Clarence Lafayette Smith, from Valmead; and Garland Triplett, from Clark's Chapel; (second row) Joe Anderson Jr., from Valmead; Lafayette Lackey, from King's Creek; Wallace Brookshire, from Gamewell; and R. E. "Ears" Wilson, from Lenoir. All were in the army and survived the war. (Smith.)

This 1938 wedding was held at the James W. George House. Weddings were once frequently held at a home rather than in a church. The wedding party members are, from left to right (first row) Mollie George Miller, Etonna Mabry George, Irene George Johnson, Nellie George Pebbles, Janelia George Crane (bride), and Samuel Houston George; (second row) James W. George, Joseph Brown George, Douglas Miller, Louis George, James Ivanhoe George, and Wilson Crane (groom). (George.)

Artist William A. Early was a North Carolina native, born in Marion in McDowell County. Early was a member of the Caldwell Arts Council, director of customer service for Bernhardt, and an artist. Best known for his portraits, he began to paint around 1946. About the subject of portrait painting, Early once said: "Likeness comes with practice. The first time there is almost total failure. . . . And the 1,000th time, we get likeness." (Caldwell.)

The four sons of Civil War veteran Marquis de Lafayette Smith are, from left to right, (first row) Robert Smith and Morgan Smith, both of Burke County; (second row) Samuel Smith, the first jailer in Caldwell County, and Marcus C. "Uncle Bud" Smith. (Gibson.)

"Before 41," a jazz group, plays in Caldwell County. Jarius Suddreth played clarinet; Man Foster was on the piano, which interestingly has a price tag attached; Freddie Simms played trumpet; Rich Scott was the drummer; and James Evert played the bass. (Hawkins.)

Capt. James Cunningham Harper is shown with his grandfather, Maj George Washington Finley Harper. The latter was born on July 7, 1834, at Fairfield in the future Lenoir. He was a graduate of Davison College. When his state called, he marched away with the 58th North Carolina Troops; by the end of the Civil War, he was a major. Harper returned to Caldwell County and became a business and civic leader. He was a member of the state legislature, established the bank of Lenoir, and was president of the Carolina and Northwestern Railroad. He died in 1921. His grandson was born on February 17, 1893, at Kirkwood. James earned a bachelor's degree from Davidson College and a master's from the University of North Carolina. During World War I, Harper enlisted in the U.S. Army and trained soldiers in South Carolina, Washington, D.C., and Virginia. After returning to Caldwell County, he worked in the family furniture business until 1924, when he became director of the Lenoir High School Band, which he ably led for decades. Harper died in 1986. Both the major and the captain are interred in the Harper-Bernhardt plot at Belleview Cemetery in Lenoir. (Caldwell.)

Four

BUSINESS AND INDUSTRY

At the Patterson School in Happy Valley, a threshing machine is being pulled by mules. The school's founder, Samuel Ledgerwood Patterson, was a celebrated state agricultural commissioner and Happy Valley resident who left his estate as an agricultural school. The school opened September 29, 1909, and the Patterson house, Palmyra, was used as a dormitory until in burned in 1922. The school was accredited by the state in 1937 and by the Southern Association of Colleges and Schools in 1955. (Patterson.)

Blue Bell, Inc., in Lenoir, pictured here, was the largest company of its kind in the world in the 1960s. The textile factory manufactured dungarees for the U.S. Navy. After World War II, the factory began producing the first Wrangler jeans, designed by Rodeo Ben, a designer for cowboy film stars. Wrangler continues to be a popular brand of jeans. (Caldwell.)

The Hoke Icard Store on Cajah's Mountain Road stocked many important staple items. On the shelves, there are a number of products still used today, including Wheaties, Arm and Hammer Baking Soda, Maxwell House Coffee, and Kellogg's Rice Krispies. The store also stocked products seldom seen on today's supermarket shelves: Hearth Club Baking Powder, Cinderella Raisins, and Duff's Hot Roll Mix. In addition to food and cold sodas, the store carried medicine and heath and beauty items. (Beane.)

Pictured here is a group of early Lenoir businesses. The business on the left is W. B. McCall's, the Lenoir Post Office is in the middle, and Dr. Alfred A. Kent Sr.'s drugstore is on the right. Dr. Kent was a Caldwell County native, attended the University of North Carolina, and then taught school prior to attending medical school. Kent ran this pharmacy from around 1904 until 1925, when he retired. (Caldwell.)

These Patterson School students are employed at the school's working farm. Patterson School students performed labor on the farm rather than paying tuition. Having students work to attend was a practice at several Appalachian schools and colleges, including Berea College and Warren Wilson College. This policy allowed students to receive vocational training and to have dignity in their work and education. The farm work was especially appropriate at Patterson, which began as an agricultural school. (Patterson.)

Gentlemen in this image are practicing an industry that dates back to Caldwell County's earliest days. Farmers raised turkeys on the abundant mast available when the chestnut trees thrived. Then they would drive their flocks of fattened turkeys to towns, drovers' markets, or railheads to transport and sell them. These drovers are also employing oxen to pull their wagon. Oxen were sturdy and useful animals employed by farmers well into the 20th century. (Caldwell.)

These employees of the Hudson Cotton Manufacturing Company were photographed in 1904, not long after the mill opened. The mill produced cotton yard and was powered by a steam engine until 1924, when converted to electricity. Capt. J. D. Moore was the first secretary-treasurer; J. O. White was general manager; Barney B. Hayes was superintendent; James F. Query was overseer of carding, Ed Harris was overseer of spinning, and J. P. Lee was night superintendent. (Caldwell.)

Smith Crossroads was on the main highway leading to and from Lenoir and was very well known. The business center contained a Ford dealership that sold both new and used cars and tractors, a service station, a motel, restaurant, barbershop, and beauty salon, along with the offices of other business firms. (Caldwell.)

Deal's Mill on Gunpowder Creek was built in the 1820s by William Deal III. This mill, one of two built by Deal, continued to run successfully until the 1930s. Mills were vital businesses in the early days of the county. In 1936, William Deal became the first postmaster at the Deal's Mill Post Office. (McRee.)

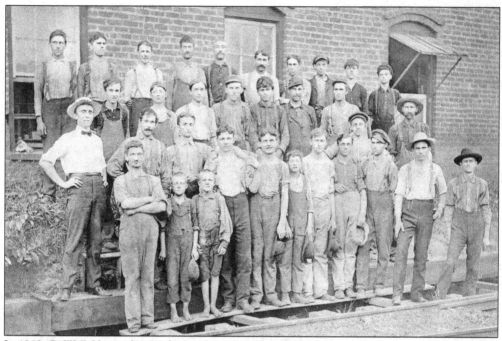

In 1889, G. W. F. Harper began the Lenoir Furniture Company. In 1899, along with G. F. Harper, J. M. Bernhardt, and G. L. Bernhardt, he reorganized the business into Harper furniture company. The company was purchased by Thomas Hamilton Broyhill and his younger brother, James Edgar Broyhill, in 1929. The two brothers worked together in their highly successful business efforts until "Mr. Tom" died in 1955. (Caldwell.)

The Gibson Store on Union Grove Road sold everything from groceries to clothing to shoes, and it even had a flower shop next door. Originally owned by John Nelson Gibson, it was the earliest store in the Cajah's Mountain area. John Nelson Gibson was a farmer and member of the Union Grove Baptist Church and the Washington Camp of Patriotic Order of Sons of America. He died in 1957, and his son Oscar L. Gibson ran the store. (Gibson.)

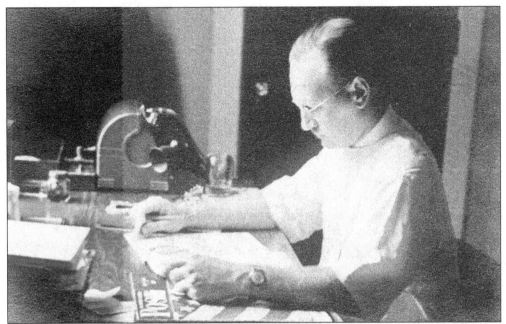

Dr. Fred M. Dula was a graduate of the University of North Carolina and the Illinois College of Ophthalmology and Otology in Chicago. In 1932, he received his M.D. from Vanderbilt University. During World War II, the surgeon and active community leader entered the navy, rising to the rank of captain in his service in the South Pacific. After the war, he returned to Lenoir. Ironically he died in 1961 while undergoing surgery. (Dula.)

In this Lenoir photograph, the logo of the Kent-Coffey Manufacturing Company can be seen on one of the buildings. This successful furniture company began April 20, 1905, with Dr. A. A. Kent and was originally the Kent Furniture and Coffin Company. After selling this business to T. H. Broyhill, Kent and Finley Coffey established the Kent-Coffey Furniture Company, which produced home furnishings and was sold to Magnavox in 1964. (George.)

Grandin, in northern Caldwell County, did not exist prior to 1912. In that year, William J. Grandin, of Tidioute, Pennsylvania, purchased 60,000 acres of timber in the Watauga-Wilkes-Caldwell County area. He established a town with a timber mill to process the wood prior to shipping it out. The boarding house, pictured here, was the first building constructed in the new town. (Hsu.)

Organized in 1906, the Bank of Granite was formed with $8,000 from the original stockholders and a small brick building. The building seen here was later built in front of the first structure and included a second floor for offices. This facility was used until 1969, when the bank built a new building two blocks to the northwest, and this building became the town hall. (Caldwell.)

Don Triplett worked for the Lenoir Furniture Corporation for over 32 years. In this photograph, taken around 1940, he is engaged in staining pieces that would become beautiful pieces of furniture. (Triplett.)

These Kent-Coffey employees are captured in a photograph taken c. 1937. The numerous furniture industries in and around Caldwell County employed a variety of people, including quite young people. The child being held by the gentleman on the left is undoubtedly just visiting the plant, but the young man on the right appears to be an employee. (Caldwell.)

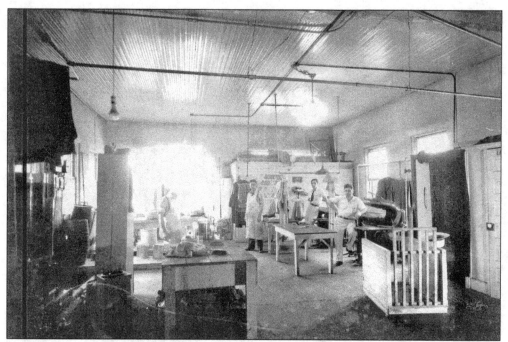

By 1927, a one-story cleaning and dying business was located in a brick building at 114 Mulberry Street. Pictured in this photograph from left to right are employees of the Piedmont Cleaners: L. D. Cook, Charles Hathcock Sr., Frank Sigmon, and Paul Broome. Piedmont Cleaners operated in this building through the 1950s. (Caldwell.)

The Hudson Veneer Company, pictured here, along with the Lenoir Veneer Company, helped supply the early furniture industry that sprang up in Caldwell and surrounding counties. The Hudson Veneer Company was established in 1915 and, by the early 20th century, under Pres. R. S. Crisp, employed 65 people. (George.)

The Civilian Conservation Corps (CCC) was established by Franklin Roosevelt in March 1933. The CCC employed men between the ages of 18 and 25 and existed until the 1940s. Men in the CCC lived in camps all over the nation, such as the one in Mortimer, and largely helped with reforestation on the logged hillsides. Here workers are rebuilding a low water bridge in Mortimer after the 1940 flood. (Caldwell.)

The Caldwell County Agricultural Building was dedicated on June 25, 1937. In 1939, the building also housed the county library and the Curb Market. A fire in December 1944 destroyed the building, but the walls were found sound and the structure was rebuilt. The library was a loss. County commissioners at the time of its construction were G. M. Goforth Jr., W. L. Minish, and P. L. Poovey. (Caldwell.)

In this image of the Bank of Lenoir, an adjacent business offers Western Union service and burial plots. The impressive facade belies the bank's humble beginnings in 1894. Its first president was Maj. G. W. F. Harper, and the original capital for the bank was a mere $10,000. A 1914 advertisement boasted that the bank had over $500,000 in assets and responsibilities. This building was demolished and a new bank building constructed on the site in 1982. (Caldwell.)

These Patterson School students are butchering hogs. Those on the right are scraping the hair from the dead hogs. The hogs on the left are scraped and in the process of being butchered. The scalding water on the right was used to assist in the removal of the hair. Well into the 20th century, pork was a staple of Appalachian diets, since the hogs were low-maintenance livestock and the smoked meat kept for months without refrigeration. (Patterson.)

The town of Collettsville was incorporated in 1897, and the first post office was established in 1937. James H. Collett owned the land where the town was established, and it was given his name. In the 1916 flood, the post office was washed across the road and came to rest on the other side, where it remained. (Beane.)

Fairfield Chair employees in 1937 are pictured from left to right as follows: (first row) Ralph Hollar, Russell Cody, Frank Conner, and Neil Beck; (second row) Al Clapp, Dick Ragsdale, Brooks Austin, Ed Bean, Gordon Smith, Arvil Hall, Milt Jackson, and Lon Ragsdale. Fairfield Chair Company was established in 1921 and continues to be a locally owned company. (Caldwell.)

The design of this building followed other courthouses in Western North Carolina designed by Charlotte architects Wheeler, Runge, and Dickey. Construction was completed in 1904, and the building had a central dome and a pedimented tetra-style portico. William A. Otter and local builder E. A. Poe were awarded the contract for the building's construction. The building was remodeled in the late 1920s. (Caldwell.)

Renovated in 1928, the Caldwell County Court House was given a new facade designed by architect Martin L. Hampton. According to a local newspaper, the building became a "stylized Neoclassical building in tan brick stone, with Art Deco influence evident in its geometric motifs." The building is located on Main Street, at the corner of West Avenue, and was enlarged and remodeled in 1990. (Caldwell.)

This aerial image of the Kinkaid Furniture Company shows the large and successful plant that began in August 1946 with Wade Kinkaid and a mere 24 employees. The company initially manufactured cedar chests and wardrobes in part of what is today Plant 1. Today the company, parented by La-Z-Boy, continues to thrive and produce beautiful pieces as the nation's leading solid wood furniture manufacturer. (Caldwell.)

The 1951 opening of Caldwell Memorial Hospital was a great cause for celebration. The 100-bed hospital was built at a cost of $1.25 million. Caldwell had a number of small hospitals beginning with Dr. Houck's unsuccessful 1899 endeavor that became the Carlheim Hotel. Caldwell Memorial Hospital continues to provide a variety of advanced medical services. (Caldwell.)

Lenoir's West Avenue Cafe was operated by two brothers, Dewey Roosevelt Icenhour and Conley Bruce Icenhour, between 1929 and 1934. The cafe was located on West Avenue between Depot Street and the Caldwell County Creamery, which was a cooperative that produced Mountain Laurel butter. (Caldwell.)

The Jones Ford Dealership in Granite Falls was one of the area's early businesses. The company began as the first Ford agency in town with its initial owner, Ed Looper, who later sold the business to M. E. Jones. Eventually the dealership was purchased by Finley Simmons, who ran the business with his son, Steve. (Caldwell.)

Early-20th-century travelers often spoke highly of the grand Carlheim Hotel, pictured here. The hotel was built in 1899 as a hospital by a Dr. Houck but was soon sold and became the Archer Hotel. Two of its most prominent owners, Charles Berry and Harry Eicher, gave the hotel the name Carlheim. The hotel closed in 1975, and the property was purchased by First Presbyterian Church, which tore down the hotel to construct the Koinonia Apartments. (George.)

Edgemont was the terminus of the Lenoir and Northern Railroad. From here, numerous spur lines went out to transport the timber that covered the area. The timber was milled and stacked, as seen here, ready to be shipped to market. Edgemont was also something of a resort town. Coaches came from Blowing Rock and Linville, bringing passengers farther into the mountains. The town even boasted the fine Edgemont Hotel and Camp Rainbow for girls. (Caldwell.)

This thriving Lenoir Standard Oil Company service station proudly carried Standard Gasoline and Mobil Oil. In addition to service provided by the men posing at the pump, the station offered easy directions with the sign out front. The sign told visitors "This is Lenoir" and gave helpful directions and mileage counts to nearby towns. (Caldwell.)

The Dudley Lumber Company was established in 1890 but destroyed by fire in 1916. Pictured in this 1885 photograph from left to right are Dudley Lumber employees (first row) Will Bolick, and Theodore Payne; (second row) L. T. Sharpe, unidentified, John Clay, Fulton Cline, unidentified, Lee Cline, two unidentified, A. M. Martin, D. H. Warlick, and Junie Turnmire; (third row) Virgil Sherrill, John Lefevers, unidentified, John Mull, C. A. "Judge" Teague, Rufus Hefner, Horton Turnmyre, and "Coot" Lefevers. (Caldwell.)

The impressive vault of the Union National Bank of Lenoir was supposedly burglar proof. The bank was organized in 1931 by several citizens, including Charles H. Hopkins, T. H. Broyhill, L. A. Dysart, John Squires, and F. H. Coffey, and boasted a large lobby with black-and-white tile as well as the crucial vault. (George.)

Stacks of lumber, destined to become furniture, abound in this photograph. In 1919, Thomas H. Broyhill became the majority owner of the Lenoir Furniture Corporation, which was manufacturing bedroom and dining room furniture. Thomas's brother started the Lenoir Chair Company in 1926, allowing the company to expand into an upholstery line. By the 1970s, Broyhill Furniture Industries had expanded to become a world leader in the furniture industry. (George.)

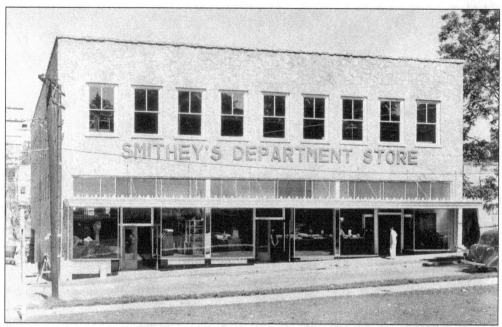

Smithey's Department Store chain began in Wilkesboro with Nikeard Bruce Smithey, who had established 17 stores, building many of them himself, by the time of his death in 1953. The Lenoir branch of Smithey's was a fixture in Lenoir for over 60 years before closing on October 27, 1994. The building was demolished in 2006. (Caldwell.)

Lenoir Chair Company started out as the Moore-Stone Company, named for its founders, Joe C. Moore and T. J. Stone. The company was purchased by Willis Shell, J. E. Shell, C. M. Pickens, and others and renamed. The factory burned, and what was left was purchased by R. C. and C. L. Robbins and became the Hibriten Chair Company. It was later acquired by Bernhardt Furniture Industries. (George.)

Alfred Bradshaw came to the Mulberry area in the early 1800s and married Charlotte (Little) Morgan. One of his descendants, Alfred Joseph (Joe) Bradshaw, owned and operated this steam-driven sawmill for a number of years. Smaller, family-owned sawmills and lumber companies were more numerous than the larger, corporate-owned entities. (Caldwell.)

The Granite Bottling Company of Granite Falls was owned and operated by H. V. Bolick and boasted "perfect sanitary conditions." In the early 20th century, the plant sold its products in four counties and bottled several popular drinks, including the still-beloved Cheerwine. Here some of the plant's bottling machinery is clearly visible. (George.)

The Ritter Lumber Company operated from 1895 until 1960, when it was purchased by Georgia Pacific. Lumber companies like Ritter leased land while conducting their timbering operations, and many had company stores, like this one. Similar to mining companies, the lumber companies often ran their business on scrip, paying workers with specially made metal or paper currency that was only good at the store, thus ensuring their employees shopped there. (Caldwell.)

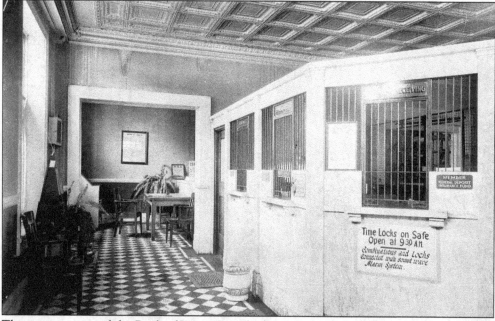

This interior view of the Bank of Lenoir reveals the cashiers' desks. When the bank was first established, there were only two cashiers. The original cashier was G. F. Harper, son of Maj. G. W. F. Harper, the bank's president. The assistant cashier was J. H. Beall. Harper soon left the bank to become involved in the furniture business; Beall succeeded him, and A. G. Ford became the assistant. (George.)

Mules were essential to successful farming. In this image, taken at the Patterson School's working farm, the mules are being used for plowing. The school's working farm allowed students to gain valuable training in their agricultural skills while also providing food and income for the school. Patterson continues to thrive as a boarding school but is no longer a working farm. (Patterson.)

Hardin Corpening Suddreth was known as "Hardie" to friends and family. His second wife, Nancy Alice Coffey, was a schoolteacher who had been his childhood sweetheart before rejecting his initial proposal in favor of her education. At the age of 21, Hardie began working in a grocery and feed store in Lenoir. He later worked at the Cloers Market, which became a branch of Carolina Stores. Here Hardie, left, stands with Gus Cloer in front of the store. (Throneburg.)

In this fragile tintype image, George Gilbert Smith and Ruhamah Smith stand proudly in front of their store in the North Catawba community. They display two bolts of fabric, some of the many items available in their business. Many Appalachian entrepreneurs ran small stores that provided much-needed manufactured goods to their communities. (Gibson.)

Students here at the Patterson School working farm are collecting dried corn stalks to make fodder shocks. Today seen as festive autumn decorations, fodder shocks were once essential for feeding livestock in the winter. These students are all boys, but in 1971, the school began admitting girls as day students and in 1981 allowed girls to board. (Patterson.)

Five

TRANSPORTATION

Horses and mules were a part of everyday life for everyone in Caldwell County prior to the popularity of the automobile. They were used to plow the fields, bring in the crops, take surplus crops to the market, and bring supplies back. Plus there were social events as well, such as church or trips to town during elections. Pictured are Philo Harmon (left), George Bolick (on horse), and Ronda Greene, all of the Mulberry community. (Greene.)

Railroads first came to Caldwell County in 1884, when a group of local investors financed the 110-mile freight and passenger line that originated in Chester, South Carolina. The narrow-gauge line was known as the Chester and Lenoir Railroad. This line also served to funnel tourists into the area, making the new resort town of Blowing Rock much more accessible. (Caldwell.)

In the early 1930s, Lenoir High School was able to acquire transportation for its soon-to-be world-famous high school band. There were passenger transports for the students as well as a large van for the instruments, as seen here. All the vehicles were painted red. This image was taken in the Mortimer community in June 1935 (Caldwell.)

Automobiles were a novelty in most rural counties until well into the 20th century. In this image, Harold Coffey drives proudly while Clyde Suddreth (left) and Willis Suddreth (back seat) ride along. Note the jaunty horn attached to the running board. (Caldwell.)

In this early-20th-century image of downtown Lenoir, a variety of forms of transportation are visible, revealing the slow transformation of transportation technology. Near the recently installed Confederate monument, a buggy is pulled by a horse and other horse-drawn conveyances are visible in the background next to automobiles and beneath the electric lines. (Caldwell.)

Lenoir has had some type of fire protection since 1877, when a bucket brigade was organized. This was replaced by a horse-drawn unit, then a 1918 four-cylinder American LaFrance engine and a 1923 American LaFrance pumper. Pictured here in 1948 is an open-topped fire truck with Smokey, the mascot, perched on top. (Caldwell.)

Train trestles were a fact of life when navigating the hilly terrain of the mountains of Western North Carolina. Here an excursion train sits atop a high trestle of the Carolina and Northwestern Railroad, near Edgemont in northern Caldwell County. Excursion trains brought groups of people, at times from as far away as Chester, South Carolina, to the mountains for a day of sightseeing. (Caldwell.)

The Grandin Lumber Company, like many lumber companies, owned and operated its own rail equipment to transport timber and finished lumber. The Grandin had two Baldwin locomotives as well as this Porter "dinky," a smaller engine used to shuttle cars loaded with logs and to operate as a yard switcher in the mill complex. (Hsu.)

Photographs often capture both the mundane and the important. Here in 1937, the camera has captured the first delivery of mail in Lenoir via airplane. Pictured from left to right are John Matterson, assistant postmaster; N. H. George, postmaster; the pilot of the airplane; and Mayor Earl Tate. (Caldwell.)

By the late 1930s, there were 38 "filling stations" in Lenoir. This station sat on the corner of Mulberry Street and Harper Avenue. The Mack truck, which had solid rubber tires, was a gasoline transport truck, and the car is a 1923 Model T-6 Rio owned by Claude Hailey. This station offered Standard Gasoline, Mobil Oil, and "Crank Case Service." (Caldwell.)

A photographer snapped this photograph on June 4, 1884, as the first engine of the Chester and Lenoir Railroad sits upon the turntable in Lenoir. Columbus Weather, wearing the white shirt and leaning out the window of the locomotive, is engineer. Capt. Hugh Waddell is in front of the locomotive, under the light. By 1893, another line, the Caldwell and Northern Railway, connected Lenoir with Collettsville. (Caldwell.)

In this image, taken near the town of Collettsville around 1911, farmers use mules and horses to transport lumber in wagons. To haul the trees in from areas without roads, sleds were often employed. In areas with roads, such as this one, wagons continued to be used long after the advent of the automobile. (Caldwell.)

Driver's education classes are now an indispensable part of most high school students' educations, but these courses require the use of a vehicle for the fledgling drivers. This car, being presented to Lenoir High School by Sanders Chevrolet Company, was a generous gift that allowed students to have hands-on experience behind the wheel and perhaps helped them avoid unpleasant curbside conversations with the police officer on the right. (Caldwell.)

A steam engine belonging to the Carolina and Northwestern shuttles freight cars. In 1903, the narrow gauge Chester and Lenoir Railroad was upgraded to standard gauge and reorganized as the Carolina and Northwestern Railroad. This line was later a subsidiary of the Southern Railway. (Caldwell.)

H. M. Teague took this picture of his automobile at the Hibriten Pavilion in June 1911. The car was the first one to reach the top of Hibriten, where dances were sometimes held. Nell Powell and Sam Tuttle sit in the front of the car and Alice Powell Henry in the back. Lee Cottrell stands on the left, while the gentlemen on the right were servers at the Dutch Lunch, held in conjunction with the North Carolina Press Association Conference in Lenoir. (Caldwell.)

In the early 1900s, there were about 2,000 automobile manufacturers, each producing one or more cars in the United States. By 1920, that number had decreased to 100, by 1929 to 44. All of these cars would need service at some point, and service stations and wrecker services, like these of the Cromwell Robbins Wrecker Service, rose to meet the demand. (Caldwell.)

J. E. Corley rode the lines for the Buffalo Power Company on old Frosty. He lived on Lizard Ridge. Many of the locations where Corley, a World War I veteran, had to go to check on the power lines were inaccessible for automobiles, but an experienced horseman would have little trouble traversing the rugged terrain. (Corley.)

It is unknown just when the City of Lenoir acquired this moped, but it undoubtedly helped with the enforcement of law and order. The officer riding the unusual law enforcement vehicle is Ronda Hagaman, pictured in the 1930s, and he is in front of a service station redone as a cab company. This structure was recently demolished. (Caldwell.)

The sight of new technologies, like airplanes, automobiles, televisions, radios, and telephones, often produced feelings of excitement and fear. On October 10, 1919, while the Caldwell County Fair was in session, this airplane made a visit. It was the first time that a flying machine was seen in Lenoir. (Caldwell.)

The livelihoods of almost all people depended upon the use of horses, mules, and oxen. Many learned to ride and used horses and mules at an early age. Here Roby Houck, age six, in 1919 sits upon a mule. Later in life, Houck would be the proprietor of Houck's Trim Shop. (Caldwell.)

Building railroads in the mountains was a difficult job. Rivers, creeks, and ravines needed to be bridged; tunnels had to be dug through mountains; lumber was cut and split into ties; rails were laid and spikes driven; and as shown in this photograph, small hills had be hollowed into cuts. This cut was made in the Edgemont-Mortimer area, and the photograph was taken in 1907. (Caldwell.)

Hardie C. Suddreth purchased this 1929–1930 black Chevrolet bus to transport the youth of the Gamewell Episcopal Methodist Church on special trips. His own children, Woodie, Mary, and Hill, used the bus as a playhouse when it was not fulfilling its intended duties. (Throneburg.)

Pictured here is the first firefighting equipment of the Lenoir Fire Department. The equipment, according to a local newspaper, consisted of "two fine stallions, Ned and Rex; a high-heeled wagon which carried a limited supply of hose . . . a half-dozen hand-axes and tools; and a nozzle or two." This equipment was later replaced by a 1914 American LaFrance model truck. (Caldwell.)

Number 102, a 2-8-0 Baldwin Locomotive Works engine, was one of two Class 10-34-E locomotives purchased to run on the Watauga and Yadkin River Railroad. The line ran out of Wilkesboro, in Wilkes County, and into Grandin, a new mill town established in northern Caldwell County. The line was extensively damaged in the floods just before 1920. (Hsu.)

This 1905 image features, from left to right, R. Berge Bush and his daughters Maggie and Beth riding in a smart buggy. Sadly Maggie was one of the nearly 10,000 North Carolinians who perished in the 1918–1919 influenza epidemic. According to her obituary in the *Lenoir News*, "the great enemy snatched from [the Bush family] their beloved daughter," an intelligent, studious young woman who lived "a consecrated Christian life" and died January 13, 1919. (George.)

Here one of the engines of the Chester and Lenoir Railroad is seen crossing the Catawba River. Many of the trains into and out of Caldwell County were mixed, having both boxcars for freight and coaches for passengers. Many of the trains leaving Caldwell County were mixed, but many also hauled the valuable timber. (Caldwell.)

With the arrival of the railroad, depots sprang up at towns and communities along the line. While the names of these two gentlemen are unknown, they are working inside the depot at Collettsville. Depots handled both freight and passengers and were usually the local telegraph offices. The telegraph can be seen in the center of the photograph, just above the "Carolina & NW" trademark. (Beane.)

Six

Clubs and Events

The Center Theatre provided entertainment to Lenoir residents before it was torn down in 1990. In 1942 during World War II, the theater kept up morale at home by playing popular films like *This Gun for Hire* while also supporting the war effort by hosting a scrap metal drive to recycle metal items into military vehicles and munitions. (Caldwell.)

The Independent Order of the Odd Fellows was a fraternal organization with some similarities to the Freemasons. The Odd Fellows organization was started in the United States on April 26, 1819, in Baltimore, Maryland. The Odd Fellows were dedicated to charitable and beneficent work. This photograph, of a group of Odd Fellows from Buffalo Cove, illustrates some of the regalia that the order wore. (Caldwell.)

Watauga County's Doc Watson was one of the celebrated performers who joined with the people of Hudson to celebrate their centennial in 2005. Despite his blindness, Doc is one of the most renowned musicians to ever come from the Blue Ridge Mountains of North Carolina. He began his career as a street musician in Lenoir. (Caldwell.)

This veterans' dinner, held in March 1950, was just one of the many events hosted at the Caldwell County American Legion building. The hall, which could seat 600 banquet guests, was used for parties, concerts, plays, and dances that brought famous bandleaders like Guy Lombardo and Jimmy Dorsey. Wrestling matches were also a popular attraction at the Dysart-Kendall Post, and Jack Dempsey refereed a 1953 match. (Caldwell.)

Members of the Lenoir Police Force, under the leadership of Chief Stan Crisp, and the local Boy Scout troop pose outside the police department/county jail on June 5, 1948. The scouts and policemen all look dapper in their uniforms. (Caldwell.)

The Caldwell Furniture Company in Valmead holds a company barbeque at the plant in the 1950s. Many of the local furniture factories encouraged activities such as picnics, ballgames, and other gatherings, which provided recreation for the employees and encouraged morale. (Beane.)

Valmead School provided a float in the Christmas parade in Lenoir in the 1950s. The Valmead School was first organized in 1901, when several schools were consolidated. In 1920, this one-room school burned, and a while a new school was being constructed, the classes met in a store building, a hosiery mill, and a church. New buildings were built in 1951, in 1962, and in 1991. (Caldwell.)

In June 1935, the Lenoir High School Band played in the Mortimer community. In contrast to their often highly regimented appearance, the students appear a bit more casual, with only some of them wearing their distinctive capes. One student, toward the back, wears a hat, but at a rakish angle. (Caldwell.)

Pictured from left to right are members of the Blue Bell Factory's baseball team in 1953: (first row) Pete Tolbert, Clyde Hightower, Gerald Lindsey, Richard Smith, Joe Miller, and Verne Williams; (second row) Clyde Sawyer, Jimmy Secreast, Vance Link, Earl Downey, and Clifford Nail. These teams often played other factory teams throughout the season. (Caldwell.)

Members of the local Grover Cleveland Club were photographed in July 1892 and are shown from left to right: (first row) W. C. Erwin, George F. Harper, N. H. Hailey, W. W. Scott, R. R. Wakefield, J. L. Nelson, W. C. Newland, and George Lynn Bernhardt; (second row) J. H. Beall, J. W. Kirby, Dr. Albert Houck, George C. Earnhardt, "Bun" Blackwell, unidentified, Angus Healan, Gus Newland, John M. Powell, and W. W. Deal. (Caldwell.)

On May 28, 1984, Caldwell County citizens gathered to dedicate a memorial to soldiers from 20th-century conflicts, including both world wars, Korea, and Vietnam. Pictured here are Mr. and Mrs. Jack Taylor, the donors. S. L. Underdown and state representative George Robinson are in the left background. The monument is across the street from the Confederate monument in Lenoir. (Caldwell.)

In 1936, Pres. Franklin Delano Roosevelt visited Asheville, and the Lenoir High School Band, seen behind the president, was on hand to provide musical accompaniment for the historic occasion. Note the microphone being held to FDR in the car to accommodate the president, who had been crippled by polio. (George.)

The Lenoir baseball team for 1904 included, from left to right, (first row) John Squire (center field), John Matheson (pitcher), Nelson Triplett (catcher), "Dump" White (substitute third baseman), Dave Clark (manager); (second row includes) Capt. C. Cortney (first base), Ed White (right field), John White (left field), Carrol Rabb (short stop), Dow Triplett (second base), and Garland Todd (third base). (Caldwell.)

Members of this Granite Falls baseball team in the 1920s were, from left to right, (first row) Dick Mackie, Rob Flowers, Will Carter, Nolan Turnmyre, Tate Jones, and Jim Whisnant; (second row) Roby Houck, Clive Payne, Cecil Hickman, Walt Stirewalt, Stan Tilley, and Stan Whisnant. (Caldwell.)

The Fifty Voice Choir, consisting of local African American children, performed as part of the 1941 Caldwell County celebration in honor of the county's 100th anniversary. The events of the centennial drew over 30,000 people. The choir was organized by Mrs. Maggie Gaither. (Caldwell.)

For much of the 19th and early part of the 20th century, bands were important parts of community gatherings. Bands marched soldiers off to war, they welcomed the local circus, and they provided inspiration when politicians arrived to canvas the electorate. The Lenoir Concert Band, made up of both boys and older men, poses with an American flag in front of the Harper, Bernhardt, and Company building in Lenoir. (Caldwell.)

In 1962, presidential candidate Richard Nixon met at the Mayview Manor with several distinguished Caldwell County citizens, a popular practice for politicians. Pictured from left to right are J. E. Broyhill, Dr. Fred M. Dula, Richard Nixon, Laura Dula, Pat Nixon, and Charles Rupurt. (Dula.)

Dr. Mary Cabel Warfield held this medical clinic *c.* 1933 at the Bailey's Camp Lutheran Church. From left to right are (first row) John Hamlet, Edwin Greene, Eula Hamlet, Katharine Hamlet, Opal Bolick, Hazel Bolick, Claude Harmon, ? Tester, Lea Hamlet, Paul Harmond, and Desmond Moore; (second row) Thurman Ford, Marcus Bolick, Dillard Harmon, Dorsie Bolick, Elsie Harmon, Alseen Harmon, Willard Harmon, Vonley Ford, and ? Tester; (third row) Alma Bolick, Fannie Bolick, Sarah Ford Harmon, Irene Harmon, Della Bolick, Myrtle Bentley Bolick, Celia Bolick, Sylvia Ford Bolick, Minnie Eldredge Trexler, Lucille Trexler, Ernest "Sonny" Bolick Jr., Virginia Moretz Bolick, ? Tester, Lula Moore Tester, Collis Moore, Lottie Murl Coffey Moore, Kenneth Moore, Edna Harmon, and Olen Harmon; (fourth row) Neal Ford, Ola Ford Jackson, C. B. Ford, and Hettie Ford. (Greene.)

Students involved in cleaning the Lenoir family cemetery at Fort Defiance pause at the grave of Gen. William Lenoir. In addition to the Revolutionary War hero and political leader, the cemetery includes several other Lenoirs, such as Civil War veteran Walter Waighstill Lenoir, who lost a leg at Ox Hill. Also buried here are the general's two granddaughters, Bessie (two) and Loula (eight) who both died during an 1877 diphtheria epidemic. (Caldwell.)

In 1901, the first brick for the new Masonic Lodge for the Hibriten Lodge No. 262 AF&AM was laid in Lenoir. Shown in this photograph are, from left to right, unidentified, C. A. Sigmon, Willis Shell, unidentified, Will Suddreth, Marcial Shell, George Lynn Bernhardt, Norvel H. Hailey, Dr. J. M. Spainhour, and Thomas F. Seehorn. (Caldwell.)

Parks Underdown was stopped, waiting for a train to pass on Saturday, June 9, 1923. Right before his eyes, he saw the big C&NW engine jump the tracks and head in his direction. Underdown jumped from his Ford when he saw the train, and while his car was damaged, no one, including Engineer McCarley, was injured. However, there were conflicting reports about the accident. (Caldwell.)

Taken on July 6, 1938, this photograph captures members of the Lenoir Camera Club. Pictured from left to right are (first row) William A. Early, W. Julias Smith, Callis Coffey, and John Payne; (second row) Linda Gassawy, Betty Miller, Laura Townsend, Laura Pulliam, and Ruth Crisp; (third row) Bill Whismark, John Houston, Jesse Robbins, Reed McMillan, Faye Bradshaw, and unidentified. (Caldwell.)

Political stumping has always been an important part of American life. Here Robert Taft is in Lenoir, the "Furniture Center of the South," attempting to gain the Republican nomination. Taft, the son of Pres. William H. Taft and a U.S. senator from Ohio, was a candidate for the Republican Party nomination for president in 1940, 1948, and 1952. (Caldwell.)

Nothing excites a community like having a celebrity come to town. In this photograph, Zebulon Baird Vance, seated in the carriage, is just leaving the depot in Lenoir. Vance is North Carolina's equivalent to Robert E. Lee or Stonewall Jackson: a war hero. Vance, from Buncombe County, was representing his district in the U.S. Congress when the Civil War came. He resigned his position and became colonel of the 26th North Carolina Troops, a regiment that included a company of Caldwell County men. In 1862, Vance was elected governor of North Carolina and successfully led the state through the war years. He would go on to serve as governor three more times after the war and eventually gained one of the two seats in the U.S. Senate, a position he occupied at his death. He is buried in the Riverside Cemetery in Asheville. (Caldwell.)

During World War II, citizens across the United States worked to conserve valuable resources for military purposes. Rubber, paper, and other materials were collected in paper drives like this one held at Lenior High School in 1943. Committed Caldwell County residents thus took an important part in the war effort. (Caldwell.)

World War II placed a strain on many previously available commodities in Caldwell County as well as elsewhere in the country. Gasoline was rationed, certain foods were unavailable, and materials such as paper were in short supply. At the 1943 paper drive pictured, residents bring a variety of paper goods to be recycled and reused. (Caldwell.)

The centennial celebration held to honor the county's 1841 founding was described by newspaper writer Tom Hamrick as the "greatest event in Caldwell's history." The four-day event included performances of *Cavalcade* (a historical pageant featuring 900 people), speeches from the governor and the second assistant postmaster, and a three-mile long parade. As shown here, the center of Lenoir was packed with local residents and visitors during the festivities. (Caldwell.)

Friday, June 3, 1910, was a monumental day for Caldwell County. Over 6,000 people were in Lenoir for the unveiling of the Confederate monument. The Steel Creek band provided inspiring music, and a host of dignitaries were on hand, including Mayor W. L. Wakefield, former mayor Lt. Gov. William C. Newland Jr., and Supreme Court Justice Walter Clark, along with 200 "grizzled" old veterans, commanded by Maj. George W. F. Harper. (Caldwell.)

William Lenoir built Fort Defiance between 1788 and 1792 in the Happy Valley area of the future Caldwell County. The house was home to the Lenoir family for many generations, and these generations are buried in the family cemetery on the grounds. The home was restored in the 1970s and today hosts many different events to celebrate the area's history. Here a group of interpreters portray men from General Lenoir's time period. (Caldwell.)

The streets of the town of Hudson were bedecked with American flags on Memorial Day in May 2003. That Memorial Day was extra special. It was the day that the Veterans' Memorial in Hudson, shown here in this photograph, was dedicated. (Caldwell.)

Members of the Caldwell chapter of the American War Mothers gather for the dedication of a plaque and trees in 1926. The identified women are (first row) 3rd from left, Mrs. N. H. Gwyn; 4th from left, Mrs. W. W. Dysart; 6th from left, Mrs. M. M. Courtney; 8th from left, Mrs. John Suddreth; 9th from left, Mrs. G. L. Bernhardt; and 11th from left, Mrs. J. L Nelson; (second row) 3rd from left, Mrs. John P. Bradshaw; and 10th from left, Mrs. Emma Lindsay. (Caldwell.)

North Carolina's most beloved minister, Rev. Billy Graham, preached to a large crowd gathered at the Mack Cook Stadium in Lenoir for the August 14–23, 1970, Foothills Crusade for Christ. During the crusade, 48,700 people attended, and nearly 1,400 came forward for prayer and counseling. Graham has preached to millions of people around the world and, 30 years after this photograph, still ministered. (Caldwell.)

Lenoir was home to several minor league baseball teams from 1939 to 1951, including the Lenoir Indians, Tar Heel League (1939); the Lenoir Reds, Tar Heel League (1940); and the Lenoir Red Sox, pictured here, part of the Blue Ridge League (1946–1947) and the Western Carolina League (1948–1951). The Lenoir Red Sox were sponsored by the New York Giants. (LeFever.)

Adelaide Dula was Little Miss Lenoir for 1960. Here she is being crowned by 1959 Miss North Carolina Bettie Lane Evans, who was also the emcee for the program, which was sponsored by the Lenoir Junior Chamber of Commerce. Four-year-old Adelaide, daughter of Dr. Fred Dula and Jennie Conley Dula, is surrounded by the other charming contestants. (Dula.)

For many communities across the state, the arrival of the railroad signaled a time of economic prosperity. The rails reached Lenoir in June 1884. A large crowd, pictured here, traveled via foot, horse, buggy, and wagon to witness the arrival of the iron horse. The railroad would continue on into the untamed wilderness of northern Caldwell County, and before a generation would pass, the great forests would be gone. (Caldwell.)

For every town and city, whether urban or rural, special events and holidays are celebrated with parades. And in each locale, there are always mainstays of the community in those parades. One of those for Lenoir was Melvin "Peanut" Hines. For many years, Hines, who owned a music store, could be seen in parades playing a calliope, a steam-powered organ commonly associated with early carousels. He is pictured here in the 1968 Lenoir Christmas Parade. (George.)

Returning World War I veterans founded the Dysart-Kendall Post Number 29 of the American Legion on returning home from the Great War. Some of the members of the post formed a band with Capt. James C. Harper, pictured center holding a baton, as the bandleader. As the veterans began to get older, marry, and have children, fewer of them had time for the post band. On March 6, 1924, the post voted, on recommendation of Captain Harper, to donate its band instruments to Lenoir High School. Harper was asked to be the high school bandleader until a permanent director could be found. He conducted the band until 1958. The Lenoir High School Band was one of the first in the state. Members of the post band who were interested in continuing in the band were given permission to keep their instruments, as long as they continued to participate in the practices at the high school. (George.)

On September 27, 1942, at 3:00 in the afternoon, residents gathered at the Center Theater for a war bonds "Bond-A-Seat" fund-raiser. Captain Harper directed the band, and Cullen Johnson was master of ceremonies. The band played marches, like "Stars and Stripes Forever." Several of the numbers, such as the national anthem and "Danny Boy," were performed with vocalists. (George.)

Students take part in a Mayday celebration at Gamewell Elementary in the 1950s. Identified are, from left to right, (first row) Karen Littlejohn, Danny Courtney Jr., Billie Jean Powell, Della Reichard, Virginia Clay, Louise White, Barbara Saunders, Judy Saunders, Myra Branch, and Hazel Saunders. The second row is unidentified. Note the old store, cars, and school buses in the background. (Triplett.)

Gov. James E. Holshouser, far right, is greeted by Capt. James C. Harper (center), John Miller, Phyliss Miller (left), and members of the famed Lenoir High School Band in 1970. Holshouser was a native of Watauga County, to the north of Caldwell, and was the first Republican governor of North Carolina since the days of Reconstruction. (Caldwell.)

This festive scene captures downtown Lenoir in all of its Christmas finery, including elaborate electric lights strung from street corners and over the Confederate monument. Lenoir, known for its Christmas festivities, has hosted many memorable Christmas parades. (Caldwell.)

In the spring of 1917, a recruiting call went out in the mountain counties of Ashe, Watauga, Wilkes, Alexander, and Caldwell. The call was for a new battery of field artillery to combat the German forces in France. The company was mustered in as Battery E, First North Carolina Light Field Artillery. Lenoir's Buford F. Williams was commissioned a captain in the new organization. This photograph shows local men in Lenoir getting ready to march off to Camp Sevier in Greenville, Tennessee. Once they joined other companies at Camp Sevier, the regiment was designated as the 113th Field Artillery and was assigned to the 30th Division. The battery was armed with French 75-mm guns and saw action at St. Mihiel, in the Argonne Forrest, and at St. Hilaire. The 113th was later a part of the Third Army of Occupation before coming home to a parade in Fayetteville. (Caldwell.)

BIBLIOGRAPHY

Alexander, Nancy. *Here I Will Dwell: The Story of Caldwell County.* Salisbury, NC: Rowan Print, 1956.

Anderson, E. Carl Jr. *The Heritage of Caldwell County, Volume I.* Winston-Salem, NC: Hunter Publishing Company, 1983.

Bisher, Catherine W., Michael T. Southern, and Jennifer F. Martin. *A Guide to the Historic Architecture of Western North Carolina.* Chapel Hill: The University of North Carolina Press, 1999.

Bumgarner, Matthew and R. Douglas Walker. *Watauga and Yadkin River Railroad.* Hickory, NC: Tar Heel Press, 2003.

Caldwell Baptist Association. *Laborers Together With God: The History of the Caldwell Baptist Association, 1885–2995.* Hickory, NC: Tar Heel Press, 2005.

Greene, Nell and Lucy Wagner. "Hudson Heritage, 1905–2005." [n.p.] 2005.

Hardy, Michael C. *A Short History of Old Watauga County.* Boone, NC: Parkway Publishers, 2006.

Harper, Margaret E. *Fort Defiance and the General.* Huntington, WV: Aegina Press, 1997.

Hawkins, John O. *The Most American Thing: A History of Education in Caldwell County, North Carolina.* [n.p.] 2001.

Lenoir Fire Department: 125 Years of Service, 1877–2002. Lenoir, NC: Lenoir Firefighters Association, 2002.

Lenoir News-Topic.

McCall, Maxine. *Etched in Granite: The History of Granite Falls, North Carolina.* Granite Falls, NC: Josten Graphics, 1999.

Scott, W. W. *Annals of Caldwell County.* Lenoir, NC: News-Topic Print, 1930.

The Tradition Continues . . . Lenoir High School Band Reunion Concert, November 8, 1997. [n.p.] 1997.